Money Talk

Empowering the Next Generation with Practical Money Skills and Entrepreneurial Mindsets

By

Richard H. Brown

A Parent's Handbook for Cultivating Financ al Literacy and Independence in Children

Disclaimer

This book is designed to provide information and inspiration about financial literacy, entrepreneurship, and parenting. The content is based on the author's experiences and research and is not intended as professional financial, legal, or psychological advice. Readers are encouraged to consult with appropriate professionals for specific guidance related to their personal circumstances.

The author and publisher are not responsible for any outcomes resulting from the application of information provided in this book. All examples are for illustrative purposes only and do not represent specific endorsements or guarantees of results.

Copyright Page

Money Talk: Empowering the Next Generation with Practical Money Skills and Entrepreneurial Mindsets

Copyright © [2024] by Richard H. Brown All rights reserved.

No part of this book may be reproduced, distributed, or transmitted in any form or by any means, including photocopying, recording, or other electronic or mechanical methods, without the prior written permission of the author, except in the case of brief quotations embodied in critical reviews and certain other noncommercial uses permitted by copyright law.

PREFACE

I grew up in a home where money was a mystery. Bills were paid—sometimes. Savings accounts didn't exist, and conversations about wealth were as taboo as discussing personal failings. My parents, like many in our community, lived for the moment, focusing on survival rather than planning for the future. As a child, I didn't know what "financial literacy" meant, but I lived every day feeling the effects of its absence.

In my teenage years, the impact of this financial ignorance became glaringly evident. I watched my family struggle with debts they didn't fully understand, miss opportunities they didn't know existed, and spiral into crises they couldn't foresee. When I left home, I carried their financial habits with me like a hand-me-down jacket that didn't fit but was all I had.

The world quickly taught me hard lessons. There were moments of humiliation—like handing over a credit card at a grocery store only to have it declined. There were sleepless nights wondering how I'd cover rent. And there were countless occasions when I envied those who seemed to know a secret about money that I didn't. The weight of those years shaped me, leaving me determined to rewrite my story.

The turning point came when I became a father. Suddenly, my financial ignorance wasn't just a burden I bore—it was a legacy I could unintentionally pass down to my children. The thought of them inheriting my mistakes, of watching them repeat the same struggles, was unbearable. That realization sparked a fire in me. I vowed to learn what I hadn't been taught and, more importantly, to teach my children the skills I never had.

Purpose of the Book

This book is my way of sharing the lessons I've learned, often the hard way, as both a single parent and someone who had to rebuild their financial life from scratch. It's for parents—single or partnered—who want to give their children a gift more valuable than any material possession: the knowledge, skills, and mindset to thrive financially.

I understand the challenges you face. You may feel overwhelmed, wondering how to teach what you're still learning yourself. You may worry about balancing the demands of parenting, work, and everything else life throws at you. This book is here to guide you through it all.

By sharing my story, my successes, and my failures, I hope to offer not only practical advice but also encouragement. If I, a father with no financial guidance and limited resources, could teach my children to understand and respect money, you can too.

The Bigger Picture

We live in a world where financial literacy and entrepreneurial skills are no longer optional—they're essential. Technology is advancing at lightning speed, industries are shifting, and traditional job security is becoming a thing of the past. Our children will face challenges we can't yet imagine, but they'll also have opportunities we never dreamed of.

Equipping them with financial knowledge and an entrepreneurial mindset isn't just about ensuring they survive; it's about empowering them to thrive. These skills teach resilience, creativity, and independence. They help children navigate the complexities of adulthood with confidence, adapt to changes with ease, and even create opportunities for themselves and others.

As a single parent, I know how daunting it can feel to take on this responsibility alone. But I've also seen the incredible impact of these lessons on my children's lives. They've not only learned to manage their money—they've learned to dream big, take risks, and bounce back from failure.

This book isn't about perfection; it's about progress. It's about starting where you are, using what you have, and making the most of every teachable moment. Together, we'll explore practical strategies, share meaningful stories, and discover how to lay the foundation for a financially literate, entrepreneurial, and empowered future for your children.

Let's begin this journey together

DISCLAIMER	**II**
COPYRIGHT PAGE	**III**
CHAPTER 1: THE VALUE OF FINANCIAL LITERACY	**1**
What is Financial Literacy?	1
The Importance of Early Financial Education	2
Personal Anecdotes: Learning the Hard Way	3
The Transformative Power of Financial Education	4
How Financial Literacy Can Change a Child's Life	5
CHAPTER 2: PARENTING SOLO—WHY IT'S STILL POSSIBLE TO TEACH BIG LESSONS	**7**
Addressing the Challenges of Single Parenting	7
Strategies for Success	9
Balancing Nurturing and Discipline	11
A Father's Perspective: Resilience and Big Lessons in Small Moments	13
Why It's Still Possible to Teach Big Lessons	14
CHAPTER 3: INTRODUCING MONEY TO KIDS	**15**

AGE-APPROPRIATE FINANCIAL LESSONS — 15
MAKING LEARNING FUN — 19
PRACTICAL TOOLS FOR TEACHING MONEY — 21
WHY STARTING EARLY MATTERS — 22

CHAPTER 4: CULTIVATING AN ENTREPRENEURIAL SPIRIT — 23

ENCOURAGING CREATIVITY AND PROBLEM-SOLVING — 23
SMALL PROJECTS AND VENTURES FOR DIFFERENT AGE GROUPS — 24
LESSONS FROM FAILURE AND SUCCESS — 25
TEACHING CORE ENTREPRENEURIAL SKILLS — 27
CREATING A SUPPORTIVE ENVIRONMENT — 29
TIPS FOR SUPPORTING YOUR BUDDING ENTREPRENEUR: — 29

CHAPTER 5: TEACHING THE BASICS OF BUDGETING AND SAVING — 31

BUDGETING 101 FOR KIDS — 31
THE CONCEPT OF "NEEDS VS. WANTS" — 33
BUILDING THE HABIT OF SAVING — 35
MAKING IT STICK — 38
WHY THIS CHAPTER MATTERS — 39

CHAPTER 6: HOW TO TEACH CHILDREN ABOUT INVESTING — 40

Tools for Early Learning	42
Teaching the Long-Term View	44
Overcoming the Fear of Risk	46
Making It Stick	48
Why This Chapter Matters	49

CHAPTER 7: ENCOURAGING RESPONSIBILITY AND GENEROSITY — 50

Building Financial Responsibility	50
Teaching Generosity and Empathy	52
Balancing Independence and Social Responsibility	54
Practical Activities to Encourage Responsibility and Generosity	56
Why Responsibility and Generosity Matter	57

CHAPTER 8: OVERCOMING SETBACKS TOGETHER — 58

Turning Failures into Lessons	58
Collaborative Problem-Solving	62
Activities to Foster Resilience and Teamwork	64
Why Overcoming Setbacks Together Matters	65

CHAPTER 9: BUILDING FINANCIAL SAFETY NETS — 67

UNDERSTANDING FINANCIAL SAFETY NETS	67
TEACHING EMERGENCY FUNDS: THE FIRST STEP TO PREPAREDNESS	68
EXPLAINING INSURANCE TO CHILDREN	69
PLANNING FOR THE UNEXPECTED	70
MISTAKES AS LEARNING OPPORTUNITIES	71
BUILDING HABITS FOR THE FUTURE	72
THE ROLE OF GENEROSITY IN FINANCIAL SAFETY NETS	72
A FOUNDATION FOR SECURITY	73

CHAPTER 10: NURTURING A GROWTH MINDSET — 74

WHAT IS A GROWTH MINDSET, AND WHY DOES IT MATTER?	74
MODELING A GROWTH MINDSET AS A PARENT	75
ENCOURAGING EFFORT OVER OUTCOMES	76
TURNING FAILURES INTO LEARNING OPPORTUNITIES	76
PRACTICAL ACTIVITIES TO FOSTER A GROWTH MINDSET	77
THE ROLE OF FEEDBACK IN GROWTH	78
BUILDING RESILIENCE THROUGH CHALLENGES	79
THE CONNECTION BETWEEN GROWTH MINDSET AND FINANCIAL SUCCESS	79
A MINDSET FOR LIFE	80

CHAPTER 11: THE POWER OF MENTORSHIP AND NETWORKING — 81

WHAT DOES A MENTOR MEAN TO A CHILD?	81
FINDING MENTORS FOR YOUR KIDS	82
THE FATHER'S ROLE AS THE FIRST MENTOR	83
NETWORKING: A SKILL THEY'LL THANK YOU FOR	84
WHY GENEROSITY MATTERS IN NETWORKING	85
OVERCOMING CHALLENGES IN MENTORSHIP AND NETWORKING	86
PLANTING SEEDS FOR A LIFETIME	87

CHAPTER 12: NAVIGATING THE DIGITAL AGE — 89

BALANCING SCREEN TIME AND REAL LIFE	90
TURNING TECHNOLOGY INTO A TOOL FOR GROWTH	90
TEACHING ONLINE SAFETY AND DIGITAL RESPONSIBILITY	91
THE PITFALLS OF SOCIAL MEDIA	92
ENCOURAGING A HEALTHY RELATIONSHIP WITH TECHNOLOGY	93
MODELING GOOD TECH HABITS	94
PREPARING THEM FOR A DIGITAL FUTURE	94

CHAPTER 13: GUIDING FINANCIAL INDEPENDENCE IN ADULTHOOD — 96

STARTING THE CONVERSATION EARLY	96

EARNING THEIR OWN MONEY	97
TEACHING ABOUT DEBT AND CREDIT	98
CREATING A SAFETY NET	99
SUPPORTING BIG DECISIONS	99
LETTING GO (BUT STAYING INVOLVED)	101

CHAPTER 14: FOSTERING A LIFELONG LOVE FOR LEARNING AND ADAPTABILITY 103

WHY LIFELONG LEARNING MATTERS	103
MODELING CURIOSITY AS A PARENT	104
ENCOURAGING CURIOSITY IN EVERYDAY LIFE	105
TEACHING ADAPTABILITY THROUGH CHANGE	106
PRACTICAL WAYS TO ENCOURAGE LIFELONG LEARNING	106
THE ROLE OF FAILURE IN LEARNING	108
CREATING A GROWTH-ORIENTED ENVIRONMENT AT HOME	108
PREPARING FOR A LIFELONG JOURNEY	109

CHAPTER 15: THE POWER OF COMMUNITY—BUILDING A SUPPORT NETWORK FOR YOUR KIDS 111

WHY COMMUNITY MATTERS	111

Creating a Network of Mentors and Role Models	112
The Role of Peers in Learning	113
Leveraging Community Programs and Resources	114
Teaching Kids to Build Their Own Network	115
Building a Legacy Through Community	117

CHAPTER 16: REFLECTING ON THE JOURNEY—TYING IT ALL TOGETHER — 119

A Foundation for Independence	121

A LEGACY OF EMPOWERMENT AND OPPORTUNITY — 126

A Future of Possibilities	126
What Success Really Means	127

Chapter 1:
The Value of Financial Literacy

What is Financial Literacy?

Financial literacy is the ability to understand and effectively use financial skills, such as budgeting, saving, investing, spending wisely, and managing debt. These aren't just skills for the wealthy or those in business—they're survival skills for everyone.

Think of financial literacy as the compass that guides us through life's monetary decisions. It's about knowing where your money comes from, how to make it grow, and how to ensure it works for you. At its core, financial literacy answers three critical questions:

1. How can I earn money?

2. How can I manage it responsibly?

3. How can I grow it to secure my future?

For children, the concepts might start small—understanding the value of a dollar, the difference between needs and wants, or the simple joy of watching their piggy bank grow. But as they grow older, these seeds blossom into larger ideas: how to create a budget, avoid debt traps, and invest for their future. The earlier they learn, the better equipped they'll be to handle the financial realities of adulthood.

The Importance of Early Financial Education

Money is a fact of life, yet it's often the one subject schools don't teach and parents avoid discussing. Many of us grew up learning about money through trial and error, often with painful consequences. But it doesn't have to be that way for our children.

Early financial education isn't just about preparing kids to avoid mistakes; it's about empowering them to make confident, informed decisions. When children understand how money works, they develop a sense of control over their futures. They're less likely to feel intimidated by financial challenges and more likely to recognize opportunities to build wealth and security.

The earlier we start, the more natural these skills become. A child who grows up learning how to save a portion of their allowance is more likely to budget effectively as an adult. A teenager who understands the basics of investing may start building wealth before their peers even consider it.

Personal Anecdotes: Learning the Hard Way

I learned about money the way many people do—through mistakes. And let me tell you, they were costly.

In my twenties, I didn't know how to budget. Payday felt like a celebration, and by the end of the week, I often found myself scrambling to cover basic necessities. Credit cards became a lifeline, and before I knew it, I was drowning in debt I didn't understand.

One moment that still haunts me happened at a bank when I tried to apply for a loan. The advisor asked about my credit score, my debt-to-income ratio, and my savings.

I stared back blankly. These were terms I had never heard, let alone understood. The look of pity in their eyes was a wake-up call. I walked out of that meeting feeling embarrassed but determined to learn what I hadn't been taught as a child.

It wasn't an easy road. I devoured books on personal finance, spent hours watching videos, and made a commitment to turn my financial life around. It took years to claw my way out of debt, build savings, and eventually create a stable financial foundation for my family. But through it all, one thought kept me going: *My children will not have to learn this way.*

The Transformative Power of Financial Education
Financial literacy has the power to change lives—mine is proof. But beyond my story, there are countless examples of families who have transformed their futures by embracing financial education.

Take the story of a friend I met during my financial journey. She was a single mother with two children and a mountain of debt. With the help of a community program focused on financial literacy, she learned how to budget, negotiate with creditors, and start a side hustle. Over time, she not only paid off her debt but also saved enough to send her children to college. Today, her eldest child runs a successful business, inspired by the lessons learned at home.

Financial knowledge isn't just about dollars and cents; it's about empowerment. When we teach our children how money works, we're not just giving them tools to survive— we're giving them the confidence to dream big and the skills to make those dreams a reality.

How Financial Literacy Can Change a Child's Life
Imagine a child who grows up understanding the basics of money. They know how to save for what they want, how to recognize a good deal, and how to say no to unnecessary spending. As they grow, they learn about the power of investing, the importance of giving back, and the discipline of living within their means.

Now imagine that same child as an adult. They're financially independent, unburdened by unnecessary debt, and confident in their ability to navigate life's challenges. They may even create opportunities for others—starting businesses, mentoring peers, or giving back to their communities.

This is the vision that drives this book. Financial literacy isn't just a set of skills; it's a mindset that opens doors to freedom, security, and possibility. By teaching our children these lessons, we're not just shaping their futures—we're shaping a better world.

Let's move forward together, one step at a time, toward a financially empowered future for our families.

Chapter 2:
Parenting Solo—Why It's Still Possible to Teach Big Lessons

Parenting solo is a unique journey, one filled with profound challenges but also immense opportunities. As a single parent, you may often feel stretched thin—limited time, resources, and energy pulling you in every direction. Yet, it's precisely in this crucible of pressure that some of the most impactful lessons for your children can emerge.

This chapter explores how to rise above the constraints of single parenting to teach your children the financial literacy and entrepreneurial skills they need to thrive. It's not just about imparting knowledge but creating a legacy of resilience, independence, and resourcefulness.

Addressing the Challenges of Single Parenting
Limited Time and Resources

For single parents, time feels like a currency even more precious than money. Between work, household responsibilities, and parenting, it may seem impossible to carve out space for lessons on financial literacy or entrepreneurship. But teaching these skills doesn't require grand gestures or formal lessons; it can happen in the rhythm of daily life.

Instead of thinking of teaching as an additional task, integrate it into your routine. Discuss budgeting while grocery shopping, explain savings goals when planning a family outing, or share stories about your workday that highlight perseverance and problem-solving.

Overcoming Emotional Exhaustion

Single parenting can take an emotional toll. You may feel overwhelmed or doubt whether you're doing enough for your children. This emotional exhaustion is natural but should not deter you. Remember, your presence, love, and effort matter more than perfection. Children often learn resilience and creativity by watching how you navigate challenges, even when you don't have all the answers.

Societal Stereotypes and Self-Doubt

Society often places unfair expectations on single parents, leading to feelings of inadequacy or guilt. Let go of the pressure to "do it all." Instead, focus on what you can control: your attitude, your priorities, and the example you set for your children. Recognize that by teaching them financial literacy and entrepreneurial skills, you're equipping them with tools that many children, even in two-parent households, never receive.

Strategies for Success
1. Leading by Example

Children learn more from what we do than what we say. If you want your kids to understand the value of money, let them see you managing it responsibly. Talk openly about your financial goals, whether it's saving for a new car, paying down debt, or investing in their education. Share your thought process when making financial decisions, even the small ones.

For example, when comparing brands at the store, explain why you're choosing one over the other: "This brand is cheaper, but the quality isn't as good. This one costs a little more, but it will last longer, which saves us money in the long run." These small moments accumulate into valuable lessons.

2. **Creating Teachable Moments in Everyday Life**
   Opportunities to teach financial literacy are everywhere:

- **Budgeting:** Let your children help plan the family budget for a special occasion, such as a birthday party or vacation. Show them how to allocate funds for different expenses and prioritize what matters most.

- **Saving:** Use a clear jar as a family savings bank. Watching the jar fill up creates a tangible connection to the concept of saving.

- **Entrepreneurship:** Encourage your kids to think of ways they can earn money, whether through a lemonade stand, selling crafts, or helping neighbors with chores. Guide them through the process of setting prices, marketing, and managing earnings.

Balancing Nurturing and Discipline

Parenting solo often means wearing multiple hats: the comforter, the disciplinarian, the cheerleader, and the coach. Striking the right balance between nurturing and discipline is critical, especially when teaching financial lessons.

1. Building Trust and Open Communication

Children are more likely to engage with financial lessons when they feel safe and respected. Foster an environment where they can ask questions, make mistakes, and share their thoughts without fear of judgment. This trust forms the foundation for meaningful conversations about money and responsibility.

3. Teaching Accountability Through Financial Lessons

Accountability is one of the most important lessons you can teach your children, and money management is an excellent way to co so. Consider these strategies:

- **Allowance with Responsibility:** Tie their allowance to specific responsibilities or goals. For instance, they could earn extra money for completing additional chores or meeting savings targets.

- **Natural Consequences:** Allow your children to experience the consequences of their financial decisions in a controlled environmert. If they spend all their allowance on a toy they later regret, resist the urge to bail them out. Instead, use it as an opportunity to discuss budgeting and decision-making.

4. **Balancing Encouragement with Realistic Expectations**

While nurturing their entrepreneurial spirit, it's essential to keep their efforts grounded in reality.

Celebrate their successes, but also use failures as learning opportunities. If a lemonade stand doesn't attract many customers, discuss what could be done differently next time—better signage, a new location, or a different product.

A Father's Perspective: Resilience and Big Lessons in Small Moments

When I first became a single parent, I worried that I wouldn't have enough time, energy, or knowledge to teach my children about money. But I soon realized that it wasn't about perfection; it was about persistence.

One of the most profound lessons I ever taught my son happened during a simple trip to the grocery store. He had $10 from his allowance and wanted to buy snacks. I showed him how to compare prices and calculate what he could afford. At the end of the trip, he proudly walked away with a small bag of carefully chosen items and even managed to save $2. That day, he learned the power of informed decision-making, and I learned that big lessons often happen in the smallest moments.

Why It's Still Possible to Teach Big Lessons

As a single parent, you may not have the luxury of unlimited time or resources, but what you do have is the ability to shape your child's perspective on money and life. You don't need to have all the answers; you just need the willingness to share your journey—flaws, mistakes, and all.

By modeling good behavior, seizing teachable moments, and fostering trust and accountability, you can empower your children to become financially savvy and resilient adults. The lessons you teach today will echo far beyond your household, shaping not only their futures but potentially the futures of generations to come.

Let's move forward into the next chapter, where we'll explore practical strategies for introducing money concepts to children at any age.

Chapter 3:
Introducing Money to Kids

Teaching kids about money might seem daunting at first. How do you explain concepts like saving, budgeting, or even investing to a child who just wants to buy candy or the latest video game? The key lies in meeting them where they are—introducing financial concepts in a way that aligns with their age, interests, and understanding of the world. This chapter provides a roadmap for parents to introduce money to children in engaging and practical ways, transforming everyday moments into lifelong lessons.

Age-Appropriate Financial Lessons

Children don't need to understand the stock market or compound interest at three years old, but they do need to grasp the basics of money: what it is, how it works, and why it matters. By tailoring financial lessons to their age, you can gradually build their knowledge and confidence.

For Young Children (3–7 Years): The Basics of Money
At this age, children are naturally curious and love hands-

on activities. Use their innate interest in the world around them to introduce simple financial concepts.

- **Coins and Counting:** Start by teaching them to identify coins and bills. Play games like sorting coins by size or counting a small pile of change.

- **The Concept of Saving:** Use a piggy bank or a clear jar to show how money grows when saved. Let them deposit coins and celebrate when the jar fills up.

- **Earning and Spending:** When they ask for toys or treats, explain that money is exchanged for goods. If they receive a small allowance, encourage them to save part of it for something special.

Example: My daughter once saved every penny from her allowance for six months to buy a doll she desperately wanted. When she finally handed over her saved money at the store, the pride on her face was priceless. That moment taught her more about patience and goal-setting than any lecture ever could.

For Preteens (8–12 Years): Building a Foundation

By this stage, kids are ready to handle slightly more responsibility. Introduce structured systems to teach them the value of money and the importance of planning.

- **Allowance Systems:** Set up an allowance tied to specific chores or responsibilities. For example, they might earn $5 a week for helping with household tasks.

- **Goal Setting:** Teach them to set financial goals. If they want a new gadget, help them calculate how long it will take to save up for it.

- **Simple Budgets:** Introduce budgeting with a "spend, save, give" system. Divide their allowance into three categories:
    - **Spend:** Money for immediate wants, like snacks or toys.
    - **Save:** Money for larger goals or future use.

- **Give:** Money to donate to charity or help someone in need.

Example: My son once wanted a remote-controlled car. Together, we created a savings chart. Every week, he added his saved allowance to the chart, watching his progress grow. When he finally bought the car, he not only appreciated it more but also understood the value of delayed gratification.

For Teens (13–18 Years): Real-World Skills

Teenagers are on the brink of adulthood, making this the perfect time to teach them practical financial skills.

- **Managing Bank Accounts:** Open a teen savings account and teach them how to deposit money, monitor balances, and use debit cards responsibly.

- **Earning Money:** Encourage them to take on part-time jobs, babysitting gigs, or entrepreneurial ventures. This not only teaches them the value of hard work but also introduces them to income management.

- **Basic Investing:** Introduce simple investment concepts like the power of compounding or how mutual funds work. Use analogies they understand, like comparing investing to planting seeds and watching them grow over time.

Example: When my oldest turned 16, I helped him set up a custodial investment account. We started small, buying shares of a company he admired. Watching those shares grow over time was a transformative experience—it turned an abstract concept into something tangible.

Making Learning Fun

Money doesn't have to be a dry or daunting subject. By turning financial lessons into games and activities, you can make learning enjoyable and memorable.

1. Financial Games and Apps

Use board games like *Monopoly* or *The Game of Life* to introduce budgeting and financial decision-making. For a digital twist, try apps like *PiggyBot* or *Greenlight*, designed to teach kids about saving and spending.

2. Hands-On Activities

- **Chore-for-Pay Systems:** Create a list of chores with corresponding payouts. For example, washing the car might earn $10, while folding laundry earns $5.

- **Lemonade Stands or Craft Sales:** Encourage entrepreneurial ventures. Let them plan, price, and sell their products, learning about costs, profits, and customer service.

4. Storytelling:

Children love stories, especially when they can relate to the characters. Share tales of your financial journey or create fictional stories about a character who learns about money.

Example: I once made up a bedtime story about a boy named Sam who wanted a magic bike. Sam had to save gold coins to buy the bike, learning about earning, saving, and giving along the way. My kids loved it, and it sparked questions about how they could save for their own "magic bikes."

Practical Tools for Teaching Money

1. Savings Jars or Digital Equivalents

The classic "spend, save, give" jars are a visual and tactile way for younger children to manage money. For older kids, consider digital tools like bank apps or family budgeting software to introduce them to modern financial management.

2. Allowance Systems

Set clear rules for allowance use, emphasizing the importance of saving a portion. Use apps like *RoosterMoney* to track their spending and savings.

3. Real-Life Scenarios

Involve your children in family financial decisions when appropriate. For example, let them help compare prices when shopping or decide how to allocate a small portion of the household budget.

Why Starting Early Matters

Introducing money to children is about more than just dollars and cents—it's about equipping them with life skills. The earlier they start learning, the more confident and competent they'll become in managing their finances.

As parents, we have the power to turn everyday moments into profound lessons. Whether it's counting coins with a preschooler or discussing investment strategies with a teenager, each conversation builds a foundation for their financial future.

In the next chapter, we'll delve into cultivating an entrepreneurial spirit, exploring how creativity and innovation can empower your children to think big and take control of their destiny.

Chapter 4:
Cultivating an Entrepreneurial Spirit

Raising children with an entrepreneurial mindset isn't just about encouraging them to make money—it's about teaching them to think creatively, solve problems, and take ownership of their goals. Entrepreneurship instills confidence, resilience, and a proactive attitude toward life. This chapter explores how parents can nurture these qualities in their children, regardless of their starting point or resources.

Encouraging Creativity and Problem-Solving

Entrepreneurship thrives on creativity and the ability to find solutions to challenges. Encouraging these traits starts with understanding your child's unique interests and strengths.

How to Identify and Nurture Interests and Strengths

- **Observe and Listen:** Pay attention to what excites your child. Do they love drawing, building things, or solving puzzles? These passions often hold the key to entrepreneurial ideas.

- **Ask Open-Ended Questions:** "What do you enjoy doing the most?" or "What problems would you like to solve in the world?" These questions can spark insights into their interests.

- **Provide Opportunities for Exploration:** Enroll them in workshops, take them to museums, or encourage hobbies that expand their curiosity and skill sets.

Example: My youngest son, Michael, loved drawing robots. One day, he came up with the idea of designing custom robot bookmarks. We printed a few designs and sold them at a school event. Not only did he discover a love for creating, but he also learned about pricing, customer feedback, and managing his "bus ness."

Small Projects and Ventures for Different Age Groups
- **For Young Children (5–8):** Simple ventures like selling lemonade, creating handmade greeting

cards, or setting up a mini "store" to trade toys with friends.

- **For Preteens (9–12):** More structured projects like baking cookies for sale, walking neighbors' dogs, or offering small services like helping with yard work.

- **For Teens (13–18):** Digital or tech-based ideas like starting a YouTube channel, creating digital art commissions, or building an online store through platforms like Etsy.

Example: My daughter, Sarah, began making scented candles in middle school. It started as a fun craft but grew into a small business when her friends and neighbors began requesting custom orders. Watching her learn about pricing materials, packaging, and customer service was inspiring.

Lessons from Failure and Success

Failure is an inevitable part of any entrepreneurial journey. Teaching children to view setbacks as learning opportunities is one of the greatest gifts a parent can offer.

Stories from Our Family's Ventures

When my son, David, was 10, he decided to sell handmade keychains at a school fair. Unfortunately, he priced them too high and only sold a few. Initially, he was disappointed, but we used the experience to talk about understanding customer needs and adjusting pricing strategies. By the next fair, he'd improved his product and made twice the sales.

Conversely, there were moments of triumph. My daughter, who loved baking, set up a cookie stall in our neighborhood during the holidays. She learned to calculate costs, market her goods with flyers, and even reinvest her profits into better ingredients. Seeing her confidence soar was a reward in itself.

Key Lessons Learned

1. **Resilience:** Failure is a stepping stone, not a dead end.
2. **Adaptability:** Be willing to pivot and try new approaches.

3. **Celebrating Success:** Acknowledge wins, no matter how small, to build momentum and motivation.

Teaching Core Entrepreneurial Skills

To foster an entrepreneurial spirit, children need practical skills they can apply throughout life. These aren't just business principles—they're life lessons.

1. **Perseverance:**

   Entrepreneurship requires grit. Teach your children to keep trying, even when things don't go as planned. Share stories of famous entrepreneurs who faced rejection or failure before succeeding, such as Walt Disney or Oprah Winfrey.

2. **Adaptability:**

The ability to pivot is critical in business and life. Encourage your children to think on their feet and come up with creative solutions when things don't go as expected.

3. **Risk-Taking:**

   Help your children embrace calculated risks by explaining the potential outcomes and how to weigh pros and cons. A small, manageable project like investing a portion of their allowance into materials for a craft project teaches them how to evaluate risks versus rewards.

4. Basic Concepts: Profit, Loss, and Reinvestment

- **Profit:** Show them how to calculate the difference between costs and earnings.

- **Loss:** Explain that not all efforts result in financial gain and why that's okay.

- **Reinvestment:** Teach the importance of using profits to improve or expand their ventures.

Example: My son used profits from his neighborhood car wash to buy better supplies, which allowed him to clean cars more efficiently and attract more customers. This simple act of reinvestment demonstrated the power of planning for growth.

Creating a Supportive Environment

Children thrive when they know they have a safety net. As a parent, your role isn't to take over their ventures but to guide, encourage, and cheer them on.

Tips for Supporting Your Budding Entrepreneur:

- Celebrate their creativity and efforts, regardless of the outcome.

- Offer guidance without micromanaging—let them make decisions and learn from the results.

- Connect them with resources, such as books, mentors, or online courses, to expand their knowledge.

Cultivating an entrepreneurial spirit in children is about more than teaching them to make money; it's about empowering them to see possibilities, tackle challenges, and think outside the box. These lessons will serve them well whether they choose to start their own business or pursue other passions.

In the next chapter, we'll delve into teaching kids the art of budgeting and saving—two foundational pillars of financial success.

Chapter 5:
Teaching the Basics of Budgeting and Saving

Financial literacy begins with the basics—understanding how to budget and save. These are skills that even many adults struggle with, yet when taught early, they become second nature to children. Budgeting and saving serve as the foundation for financial independence, and teaching these concepts doesn't have to be complex. With the right tools, techniques, and patience, you can empower your child to master money management.

Budgeting 101 for Kids
What is Budgeting?

Budgeting is simply a plan for how to use money. It's a skill that helps children understand where their money comes from (income), where it goes (expenses), and how to keep track of both.

1. **Explaining Income, Expenses, and Tracking**

    - **Income:** For kids, income might come from an allowance, earnings from small jobs, or gifts. Explain that income is the total amount of money they receive.

- **Expenses:** Help them categorize expenses, such as snacks, toys, or contributions to a class project.

- **Tracking:** Introduce a system for tracking money. It could be as simple as a notebook where they write down how much they've spent and saved or as advanced as using a budgeting app designed for kids.

2. **Practical Activities to Teach Budgeting**

    - **The Envelope Method:** Give your child three envelopes labeled "Spend," "Save," and "Give." Each time they receive money, guide them to allocate it among the envelopes based on agreed-upon percentages, such as 50% for spending, 40% for saving, and 10% for giving.

- **Create a Mini-Budget:** For older kids, provide a set amount of "income" and a list of potential expenses. Ask them to prioritize how they'd spend the money, helping them see the importance of planning.

- **Use a Budgeting App:** Apps like "RoosterMoney" or "GoHenry" are child-friendly tools that make tracking income and expenses interactive and engaging.

3. **The Weekly Check-In:**

Dedicate time each week to sit with your child and review their spending and saving habits. This can be a fun bonding experience while reinforcing accountability and the importance of staying organized.

The Concept of "Needs vs. Wants"
One of the most critical budgeting lessons is distinguishing between needs and wants. This helps children develop a sense of financial discipline and make thoughtful spending choices.

1. **What Are Needs and Wants?**

    - **Needs:** These are essentials like food, clothing, and school supplies—things required for survival and daily life.

    - **Wants:** These are extras like toys, video games, or trendy sneakers—things that are nice to have but not essential.

2. **Practical Exercises to Teach the Difference:**

    - **The Sorting Game:** Create a list of items (e.g., pizza, a new phone, water, school bag, candy). Have your child sort these into "needs" and "wants" and explain their reasoning.

    - **Grocery Store Challenge:** At the store, ask your child to identify items that are needs (e.g., bread) and items that are wants (e.g., cookies). This real-world application helps cement the concept.

3. **Teaching Delayed Gratification:**
   - **What It Means:** Delayed gratification is the ability to wait for something better instead of choosing immediate satisfaction.
   - **How to Teach It:** If your child wants a new toy, encourage them to save for it instead of buying it immediately. Explain how waiting and saving can lead to a bigger reward.

Personal Anecdote:

When my daughter Emily wanted a trendy doll, I suggested she save part of her allowance for it. Initially, she was frustrated, but over time, she saved enough and bought the doll herself. The pride and satisfaction she felt in achieving her goal taught her the value of patience and planning better than any lecture could.

Building the Habit of Saving

Saving is the cornerstone of financial health. By instilling this habit early, children learn to prepare for future needs and wants, manage emergencies, and build a sense of security.

1. **Setting Savings Goals:**

    - **Make It Specific:** Instead of just "saving money," encourage children to save for a specific item or experience, such as a toy, a new game, or a special trip.

    - **Break It Down:** Help them calculate how much they need to save and how long it will take. For example, if a child wants a $50 toy and saves $5 per week, it will take 10 weeks.

2. **Introducing Interest and Compounding in Kid-Friendly Terms:**

    - **What is Interest?** Explain that when they save money, it can grow over time. Use an example like, "If you save $10 and someone gives you $1 extra every month, by the end of the year, you'll have $22!"

- **The Magic of Compounding:** Show how money grows faster when they save consistently. For instance, "If you save $10 every month for a year and earn $1 in interest every month, you'll end up with more than $120!"

3. **Practical Saving Tools:**

    - **Savings Jars:** Use jars labeled "Short-Term Savings," "Long-Term Savings," and "Giving." This physical method makes saving tangible and relatable.

    - **Digital Savings Accounts:** For older kids, consider setting up a custodial savings account or using apps that simulate banking experiences.

    - **Savings Challenges:** Create fun challenges like "Save $1 a Day for 30 Days" and reward them when they complete it.

4. **Celebrating Savings Milestones:**

When your child reaches a savings goal, celebrate their achievement. This could be as simple as a congratulatory note or allowing them to enjoy the fruits of their savings, like buying the item they worked so hard for.

Making It Stick

Consistency is key when teaching budgeting and saving. Reinforce these lessons through repetition, positive reinforcement, and ongoing conversations. Remember, these are life skills that your child will rely on well into adulthood.

1. **Lead by Example:** Show your child how you manage your own budget and savings. If they see you tracking expenses or saving for a goal, they'll be more likely to emulate your behavior.

2. **Encourage Questions:** Create a safe space for your child to ask questions about money, no matter how simple or complex.

3. **Revisit Goals:** As your child grows, their financial needs and goals will change. Adapt your approach to keep them engaged and challenged.

Why This Chapter Matters

Teaching kids how to budget and save empowers them to take control of their finances early in life. It instills a sense of responsibility and prepares them to navigate a world where financial literacy is more important than ever. These lessons create a foundation that allows children to grow into confident, independent adults who make informed financial decisions.

In the next chapter, we'll dive into the world of **investing**—introducing children to the power of compounding, risk versus reward, and how to make money work for them.

Chapter 6:
How to Teach Children About Investing

Investing can seem like an overwhelming and abstract concept, especially for children. However, teaching kids the basics of investing early on can provide them with invaluable tools for building wealth and achieving financial freedom. This chapter breaks down the essentials of investing into bite-sized, relatable lessons that make it engaging and easy to understand. By simplifying concepts and using practical tools, you can help your child grasp the long-term benefits of smart investing and develop habits that will serve them for a lifetime.

Simplifying Investments

What is Investing?

At its core, investing is about putting money to work to make more money over time. Explain it to children as "using money to grow money," much like planting a seed that grows into a tree that bears fruit.

1. **Explaining Stocks, Bonds, and Mutual Funds with Relatable Analogies**

    o **Stocks:**

    Use the analogy of a pizza. Imagine a company as a pizza, and each slice represents a small piece (a stock) of that company. By buying a slice, they own part of the pizza and share in its success if it grows bigger and tastier (i.e., the company becomes more valuable).

    o **Bonds:**

    Explain bonds as lending money to someone (like a friend or the government) in exchange for them paying you back later with a little extra (interest).

    o **Mutual Funds:**

    Describe mutual funds as a big basket that collects money from lots of people to buy a mix of slices (stocks) or loans (bonds). This spreads out the risk, so no one loses too much if one company doesn't do well.

2. **Relating Investment to Familiar Activities:**

    o **Growing Plants:** Compare investing to planting a seed that takes time, water, and sunlight to grow into a tree that eventually bears fruit. This analogy helps children understand the importance of patience.

    o **Team Sports:** Explain how teamwork (diversification) in a mutual fund reduces risk because not every player (stock) has to perform well for the team to succeed.

Tools for Early Learning

Investing isn't just for adults. Today's technology offers many tools to introduce children to investing in a way that's interactive and educational.

1. **Custodial Accounts:**

- Open a custodial investment account (like a UGMA/UTMA account in the U.S.) where children can own stocks, bonds, or ETFs under a parent's guidance.

- Let them pick companies they recognize and love, such as Disney, Apple, or Nike, so they feel a personal connection to their investments.

2. **Educational Platforms and Simulators:**

    - Use kid-friendly apps like "Greenlight," "BusyKid," or "Acorns Early" to teach children about real-world investing.

    - Try investment simulators like "The Stock Market Game," which allows children to practice buying and selling stocks with virtual money in a risk-free environment.

3. **Case** **Studies:**
Share stories of how the author introduced investing to their children. For example:

- When my son wanted a new gaming console, I suggested he invest in the company that made it. We researched together, bought a few shares, and tracked its progress. Over time, he saw his investment grow, which made him more excited about saving and investing.

4. **Investing as a Family Activity:**
   - Schedule "investment nights" where the family discusses potential stocks or funds to invest in. This creates an engaging way to learn and bond over financial goals.

Teaching the Long-Term View

The most critical lesson in investing is understanding the power of time and patience.

1. **The Power of Compounding:**
   - Explain compounding in simple terms: "When you earn money on your money, and

then earn money on that money again, it starts growing faster and faster."

- Use visual examples like stacking Lego blocks: The first layer builds slowly, but as you keep stacking, the tower grows taller at a quicker pace.
- Show how $100 invested today can grow to thousands over decades, especially when reinvesting dividends.

2. **Relating Investment Growth to Real-Life Milestones:**

   - Help children understand why investing is important by tying it to their goals:
     - Saving for college: Show how a small investment now can cover part of their tuition later.
     - Buying their first car: Demonstrate how consistent investments over their

teenage years could help them afford a car by 18.

- Future freedom: Explain how long-term investing can give them the freedom to do what they love without worrying about money.

3. **Patience as a Superpower:**

    o Share a story about a child investor like Warren Buffett, who started young and benefited from years of compounding.

    o Use relatable examples: "Imagine you're baking a cake. If you open the oven too early, the cake won't rise. Investing is the same—it needs time to grow."

Overcoming the Fear of Risk

Many adults hesitate to invest because of the fear of losing money. Teaching children about risk and how to manage it early helps build their confidence.

1. **What is Risk?**

    o Risk is the chance of losing money, but it's also what makes investing exciting. Compare it to riding a bike—there's a chance of falling, but with practice and the right gear, you can enjoy the ride safely.

2. **How to Minimize Risk:**

    o Teach them about diversification (not putting all their eggs in one basket).

    o Explain the importance of researching companies and industries before investing.

3. **Handling Losses:**

    o Share stories of losses the author experienced and the lessons learned. For example:
    "I once invested in a trendy new company without doing my research. When the company didn't do well, I lost money. That

experience taught me the importance of studying before making decisions."

- Reassure children that losses are part of the learning process and that they'll get better with time and experience.

Making It Stick

Consistency and hands-on experience are key to helping children internalize these lessons.

1. **Track Progress Together:**

    - Use charts or apps to show how their investments are growing over time.
    - Celebrate milestones, like earning their first dividend or reaching a savings goal.

2. **Revisit and Adjust Goals:**

    - As children grow, revisit their goals and help them adjust their investment strategies accordingly.

3. **Keep the Conversation Alive:**

- Regularly discuss investing at the dinner table or during family meetings.
- Encourage them to read age-appropriate books or watch videos about investing to deepen their knowledge.

Why This Chapter Matters

Teaching children about investing goes beyond just money; it's about teaching them how to plan for the future, take calculated risks, and make informed decisions. By breaking down complex concepts into relatable lessons and providing hands-on tools, you equip your child with the confidence and skills to grow their wealth and achieve financial independence.

In the next chapter, we'll explore **how to protect wealth and secure financial health**—covering essential topics like risk management, insurance, and financial safety nets.

Chapter 7:
Encouraging Responsibility and Generosity

Raising financially literate children isn't just about equipping them with skills to grow their wealth—it's also about instilling values of responsibility and empathy. Money can be a tool for creating positive change, both in their lives and in the lives of others. This chapter explores how to teach children accountability in managing money, encourage them to give back to their communities, and balance their financial independence with a sense of social responsibility.

Building Financial Responsibility

Teaching financial responsibility starts with helping children understand that every choice has consequences—both positive and negative. This lesson empowers them to make thoughtful decisions with their money.

1. **The Importance of Accountability and Tracking Spending**

- **The Habit of Recording:** Introduce the practice of tracking income and expenses, no matter how small. For young children, this could be as simple as writing down their allowance and what they spend it on. For older kids, apps like "RoosterMoney" or spreadsheets can make tracking engaging.
- **Weekly Reviews:** Set aside time each week to review their spending together. Discuss what they did well and where they could improve.
- **The Power of Reflection:** Teach them to ask questions like: "Was this purchase worth it?" "Did it help me reach my goals?"

2. **Allowing Small Mistakes as Learning Opportunities**

- Let children experience minor financial setbacks, like spending all their allowance too quickly and not having enough for something they really want.

These moments can teach the value of planning ahead and resisting impulsive spending.
- Share your own stories of financial mistakes and what you learned from them. For example: "When I was younger, I spent all my first paycheck on clothes, and then I didn't have enough to pay for a dinner I promised to treat my mom to. That moment taught me the importance of budgeting."

3. **Incorporating Consequences:**
    - Introduce natural consequences to reinforce accountability. If a child spends their entire budget on toys, explain they'll have to wait until the next allowance to buy anything else.

Teaching Generosity and Empathy

Money is not just for personal gain—it can also be a powerful tool to make the world a better place. Teaching children about generosity helps them see the bigger picture and cultivates a sense of empathy for others.

1. **Incorporating Philanthropy into Financial Lessons**

- Introduce the concept of giving as part of their financial plan. Use the "spend, save, give" model to allocate a portion of their money for charitable causes.
- For younger children, this could mean donating a few coins to a local shelter. For older children, it might involve volunteering or organizing fundraisers for causes they care about.
- Use real-life examples to show the impact of giving, like funding school supplies for underprivileged children or donating to disaster relief efforts.

2. **Encouraging Children to Support Causes They Care About**

- Help them identify causes that resonate with their interests, such as animal welfare, environmental conservation, or helping local communities.
- Make the process interactive by involving them in researching charities or organizations. For

example:

"You love animals. Let's find a rescue shelter that helps stray dogs and see how we can contribute."

- Encourage creative giving, such as donating a portion of profits from a small business or organizing community drives.

3. **Storytelling as a Teaching Tool:**
    - Share inspiring stories of young philanthropists, such as kids who started their own charities or made significant contributions through small acts of kindness.

Balancing Independence and Social Responsibility

Teaching financial independence is important, but it should be coupled with an understanding of how personal choices can impact others. Social responsibility adds depth to financial literacy, turning children into compassionate, well-rounded individuals.

1. **How Financial Literacy Equips Children to Contribute Positively**

- Financially literate individuals are better equipped to support their communities, whether through personal contributions or innovative solutions to social problems.
- Encourage entrepreneurial projects with a social mission. For example:

  - Organizing a bake sale where proceeds go to a local food bank.
  - Starting a recycling program and using the money earned to fund school activities.

2. **Teaching the Ripple Effect of Money Choices**

- Show children how their spending and saving habits affect others. For instance, buying from small businesses supports local families, while wasteful spending can lead to financial strain.
- Highlight the interconnectedness of society and how small, thoughtful actions can lead to significant changes.

3. **Celebrating Social Contributions:**

- Acknowledge and celebrate their contributions to social causes. Positive reinforcement encourages them to keep giving and finding ways to make a difference.

Practical Activities to Encourage Responsibility and Generosity

1. **Family Giving Challenge:**
   - Set a family goal to support a cause together. Each member contributes a portion of their earnings or savings. This fosters teamwork and highlights the joy of collective giving.

2. **Spending Journals with a Twist:**
   - Ask children to categorize their spending into "personal use," "family support," and "community impact." This helps them see how they allocate their resources.

3. **Role-Playing Scenarios:**

- Create role-playing games where they must decide how to budget for themselves and a friend in need. This teaches empathy and practical problem-solving.

4. **Community Volunteering:**
    - Pair financial lessons with hands-on volunteering experiences, such as helping at a food bank or participating in charity events.

Why Responsibility and Generosity Matter

Teaching responsibility and generosity goes beyond money management—it builds character. Children learn to take ownership of their decisions, recognize the value of helping others, and contribute to a better world. These lessons ensure they grow not just as financially savvy individuals, but as compassionate and thoughtful citizens.

In the next chapter, we'll delve into **building a safety net and understanding financial risk**, exploring how to teach children the importance of protection, insurance, and planning for unforeseen challenges.

Chapter 8:
Overcoming Setbacks Together

Setbacks are an inevitable part of life, but they also offer some of the richest opportunities for growth. Whether it's a financial mistake or an unexpected hardship, learning to navigate challenges builds resilience and teaches lifelong problem-solving skills. This chapter explores how to turn failures into teachable moments, offers encouragement for parents who feel they're starting late, and emphasizes the value of working as a team to overcome obstacles.

Turning Failures into Lessons

Failure is often seen as something to avoid, but in truth, it's one of the most effective teachers. By normalizing failure and reframing it as a stepping stone to success, parents can teach their children to approach challenges with courage and curiosity.

1. **Sharing Personal Stories of Financial Mistakes**

   - Be open about your own setbacks. For instance:

- "There was a time I maxed out a credit card without a plan to pay it off. It took me years to recover, but it taught me the importance of budgeting and living within my means."
    - Stories like these humanize the experience of failure, showing children that mistakes are not the end but rather an opportunity to learn.

2. **Teachable Moments from Mistakes**
    - Use real-life situations to impart lessons. For example:
        - If a child spends all their allowance on a toy and can't afford something else they want, help them reflect on the consequences of impulsive spending.
        - If a family financial goal is delayed due to unforeseen expenses, explain how adjustments can be made and

what could be done differently next time.

3. **Encouraging Resilience and Adaptability**

    - Teach children to view setbacks as temporary. Reinforce the idea that perseverance can lead to solutions. For example:
        - If their small business idea doesn't succeed, help them analyze what went wrong and brainstorm new approaches.
    - Praise their efforts and problem-solving rather than solely focusing on outcomes.

For Parents Feeling "Behind"

Many parents may feel they've started too late in teaching financial literacy or entrepreneurship. However, it's important to remember that it's never too late to start. Every step forward is progress.

1. **Practical Advice for Catching Up**

    o   Start with simple actions:

    - Create a family budget together.

    - Open a savings account or start a small investment, even if it's modest.

    o   Use resources tailored for beginners, such as apps, books, or community financial literacy programs.

2. **Reassuring Parents It's Never Too Late**

    o   Highlight examples of people who achieved financial success later in life. Share stories of late bloomers who turned their situations around with persistence and determination.

    o   Emphasize the value of quality over quantity. A few impactful lessons can make a big difference, even if they're learned later in childhood or adolescence.

3. **Building Confidence in Parenting Through Setbacks**

    o Acknowledge that no parent is perfect. What matters most is showing children how to approach challenges with a growth mindset.

Collaborative Problem-Solving

Teaching financial skills isn't a solo mission—it can and should involve the entire family. By creating a team-oriented approach to setbacks, parents can foster trust, unity, and shared responsibility.

1. **Involving Children in Family Financial Discussions**

    o Age-appropriate participation:

        - Younger children can help plan grocery shopping within a budget.

        - Older kids and teens can participate in discussions about saving for family vacations or managing unexpected expenses.

- Transparency about challenges:
    - Without overwhelming children, share some of the realities of family finances. For example:
        - "We're cutting back on dining out this month so we can save for a new refrigerator."

2. **Teaching Collaborative Decision-Making**
    - Create opportunities for children to contribute ideas:
        - If the family is saving for a goal, ask them for suggestions on how to reduce expenses or earn extra money.

- For example, they might propose hosting a yard sale or taking on extra chores for a small reward.
    - Discuss the trade-offs and consequences of each decision, helping them understand the importance of prioritizing and compromise.

3. **Building a Team Mindset**
    - Frame challenges as problems the family can solve together:
        - "We're all in this together. Let's figure out how we can make it work."
    - Celebrate collective successes, whether it's reaching a savings goal or overcoming a tough financial month.

Activities to Foster Resilience and Teamwork
1. **Role-Reversal Scenarios:**
    - Let children play the role of the "family financial planner." Give them a hypothetical

budget and ask how they would allocate funds to meet the family's needs and goals.

2. **Family Brainstorming Sessions:**
   - Host monthly meetings to discuss ways to save money or generate extra income. This makes children feel valued and included.

3. **"What If" Challenges:**
   - Create scenarios where they must think creatively to handle setbacks, such as:
     - "What if we had an unexpected car repair bill? How could we adjust our budget?"

Why Overcoming Setbacks Together Matters

Every family faces challenges, but the way these challenges are handled can shape a child's perspective for life. When setbacks are addressed with transparency, resilience, and collaboration, children learn to see obstacles not as insurmountable barriers but as opportunities to grow and innovate.

In the next chapter, we'll explore **building financial safety nets**—teaching children about emergency funds, insurance, and planning for the unexpected. These skills provide a crucial foundation for long-term security and peace of mind.

Chapter 9:
Building Financial Safety Nets

Preparing for Life's Unexpected Moments

Life is unpredictable, and everyone, including children, needs to learn how to prepare for challenges that can disrupt financial stability. A financial safety net—such as an emergency fund, insurance, or a plan for unexpected events—can mean the difference between stability and crisis. Teaching children the importance of these tools not only equips them with practical skills but also instills confidence and resilience as they face life's uncertainties.

Understanding Financial Safety Nets

A financial safety net acts as a buffer against unforeseen events, like an unexpected medical bill, a car breakdown, or even a job loss. Teaching children to prepare for these scenarios early ensures they grow up with a sense of responsibility and foresight. For example, just as a child learns to pack an umbrella when the weather forecast predicts rain, they can learn to set aside money for unexpected financial storms.

To explain this to children, relate it to th ngs they care about. Ask, "What would you do if your bike got a flat tire and you didn't have the money to fix it?" Starting with relatable scenarios helps them understand the value of being prepared without overwhelming them with adult-level complexities.

Teaching Emergency Funds: The First Step to Preparedness

An emergency fund is a pool of money set aside specifically for unexpected expenses. For children, this concept can be simplified: it's like keeping extra lunch money in case their main allowance runs out.

Start by introducing the idea of saving for emergencies using small, achievable goals. Younger children can save coins in a jar labeled "Rainy Day Fund." For older kids and teens, encourage them to save a portion of their allowance or earnings into a digital savings account. It's important to stress that this money isn't for impulsive purchases—it's reserved for true needs.

When teaching this, give real-world examples. Share how you or someone else benefited from having an emergency fund: "Last year, the car broke down, and because we had an emergency fund, we didn't have to borrow money to fix it." Stories like these help children see the tangible benefits of planning ahead.

Explaining Insurance to Children

Insurance is another crucial aspect of financial safety nets, and while it may seem complex, it can be explained in relatable terms. Start by describing insurance as a way to share the financial risk of big, unexpected problems. For example, you might say, "Insurance is like everyone in the neighborhood pitching in to help rebuild a house if it catches fire. If it's your house, the group helps you, and if it's someone else's, you help them."

Introduce children to the basic types of insurance they might encounter in the future, such as health insurance, car insurance, or even renter's insurance. Use visuals or simple analogies to explain key terms like premiums, deductibles, and claims. For instance, you could say,

"Paying your premium is like putting a little money into a jar every month so that if something big happens, the jar can help cover the costs."

Engage them with activities to make learning interactive. Role-playing games, for example, can demonstrate how insurance works. Pretend your child owns a lemonade stand, and you're the "insurance company." Have them pay a small premium and discuss how it helps when their stand gets damaged in a pretend storm

Planning for the Unexpected

Preparing for unexpected events goes beyond saving money—it involves teaching children to anticipate challenges and think critically about solutions. Start with everyday scenarios to make this concept relatable. Ask questions like, "What if the power goes out and we lose the food in the fridge? How could we prepare for something like that?" Encourage them to brainstorm ideas, fostering a proactive and problem-solving mindset.

Involving children in family financial discussions can also deepen their understanding. For instance, during a budgeting session, explain how you set aside money for emergencies and ask for their input. Let them see how these decisions create stability for the household. This collaborative approach not only teaches financial skills but also strengthens their sense of responsibility and belonging.

Mistakes as Learning Opportunities

Even the best safety nets can fall short in the face of certain challenges, and when this happens, it's an opportunity for growth. If your family faces a financial shortfall due to an unexpected expense, involve your children in the solution. For example, explain why the emergency fund wasn't enough and discuss what steps you'll take to recover. By framing setbacks as learning experiences, you teach children resilience and adaptability.

Use your own mistakes as teachable moments. Share stories of times when you didn't have a safety net and how you worked to overcome the challenges. This openness helps children understand that it's okay to make mistakes as long as they learn from them and improve.

Building Habits for the Future

Creating a financial safety net is not just about saving money—it's about instilling habits that children will carry into adulthood. Encourage them to consistently set aside a portion of their allowance or earnings for emergencies. Teach them to review their savings goals periodically and adjust as needed.

For teens, introduce more advanced topics like investing as a secondary safety net or using insurance effectively in their future lives. Discuss real-life milestones, such as saving for college or their first car, to help them see how their current habits can lead to long-term benefits

The Role of Generosity in Financial Safety Nets

Finally, while safety nets are about protecting oneself, they also provide the means to help others in need. Teach children that being financially prepared allows them to be generous without compromising their stability. For instance, discuss how part of an emergency fund can sometimes be used to support friends or family in crisis, fostering empathy and social responsibility.

A Foundation for Security

Teaching children about financial safety nets equips them with the skills to face life's uncertainties with confidence and independence. These lessons go beyond money—they build resilience, encourage critical thinking, and foster a sense of security. By instilling these values early, you're preparing your children not just to survive unexpected challenges, but to thrive in spite of them.

The next chapter will delve into nurturing a **growth mindset**—empowering children to embrace challenges, learn from failures, and continuously seek personal and financial **growth**

Chapter 10:
Nurturing a Growth Mindset

Empowering Children to Embrace Challenges and Learn from Failures

A growth mindset is the belief that abilities and intelligence can be developed through effort, learning, and persistence. It's the foundation of resilience and the drive to improve—a crucial trait for personal and financial success. Teaching children to view challenges as opportunities rather than setbacks equips them to tackle problems with confidence and creativity, no matter what life throws their way.

What Is a Growth Mindset, and Why Does It Matter?

A growth mindset contrasts with a fixed mindset, where people believe their abilities are static and unchangeable. With a growth mindset, children understand that failure isn't the end—it's part of the learning process. This perspective fosters curiosity, adaptability, and grit, all essential traits in a world that values innovation and resilience.

For instance, when children encounter financial or entrepreneurial challenges, a growth mindset helps them analyze what went wrong, adjust their strategies, and try again. Whether it's a failed savings goal or an unsuccessful business venture, the ability to bounce back stronger is a lifelong asset.

Modeling a Growth Mindset as a Parent

Children often learn by example, and parents play a key role in shaping their mindset. Share your own experiences of overcoming obstacles, highlighting the steps you took to improve and the lessons you learned. For example, if you faced financial struggles, talk openly about how you adjusted your budget, learned new skills, or sought advice to overcome those challenges.

When your child faces setbacks, resist the urge to fix the problem immediately. Instead, guide them to reflect on the situation, identify what could have been done differently, and brainstorm solutions. Encouraging this process shows them that setbacks are temporary and solvable.

Encouraging Effort Over Outcomes

One way to foster a growth mindset is to shift the focus from results to effort. Praise your children for their determination, creativity, and perseverance rather than solely for their achievements. For example, if they successfully save for a goal, celebrate not just the accomplishment but the discipline and consistency it took to get there.

Conversely, when they fail to meet a goal, emphasize the value of the effort they put in and help them analyze what can be improved. This approach teaches children that success is a journey, not a fixed destination.

Turning Failures into Learning Opportunities

Failure is often seen as something to avoid, but it's one of the best teachers. Help your children view failures as stepping stones to success. For instance, if your child starts a small business selling crafts and struggles to find customers, encourage them to evaluate why. Were the prices too high? Did they target the wrong audience? Guide them to adjust their strategy and try again.

Share stories of famous individuals who turned failures into success. For example, Thomas Edison famously said about his invention process, "I have not failed. I've just found 10,000 ways that won't work." Relatable examples like this inspire children to see setbacks as part of the growth process.

Practical Activities to Foster a Growth Mindset

1. **Reflection Journals:** Encourage your children to maintain a journal where they record challenges they faced, how they addressed them, and what they learned. Reviewing these entries over time shows them how much they've grown.

2. **Goal-Setting Exercises:** Teach them to set realistic goals and break them into smaller, manageable steps. Celebrate milestones along the way, emphasizing the effort it took to achieve them.

3. **Problem-Solving Challenges:** Present hypothetical scenarios and brainstorm solutions together. For instance, "What would you do if you

lost all your saved money?" or "How would you market a lemonade stand in a crowded park?"

4. **Growth Mindset Media:** Introduce books, videos, or games that reinforce the idea of persistence and learning. Stories where characters overcome obstacles inspire children to adopt a similar outlook.

The Role of Feedback in Growth

Constructive feedback is a cornerstone of the growth mindset. Teach children to seek and embrace feedback, whether it's from teachers, peers, or family members. Frame feedback as a tool for improvement rather than criticism. For example, if a teacher suggests a way to improve their essay, emphasize that this is an opportunity to grow, not a judgment of their abilities.

Additionally, show them how to give themselves feedback. After completing a project, ask them reflective questions like:

- What went well?
- What didn't go as planned?

- What would you do differently next time?

Building Resilience Through Challenges

Resilience is the ability to recover from difficulties, and it's a skill that can be cultivated through practice. Encourage your children to take on challenges that push them out of their comfort zones. Whether it's learning a new skill, entering a competition, or managing a larger responsibility, these experiences build confidence and perseverance.

Let them struggle a little before stepping in to help. Struggling is not failure; it's an essential part of learning. When they overcome a challenge on their own, they gain a sense of accomplishment that no external reward can provide.

The Connection Between Growth Mindset and Financial Success

A growth mindset has a direct impact on financial success. It helps children approach money matters with curiosity and adaptability. For example, they might experiment with different ways to save money, analyze why certain strategies work better than others, and continually refine their approach. In entrepreneurship, a growth mindset allows them to pivot when faced with challenges, ensuring long-term success despite short-term setbacks.

A Mindset for Life

Cultivating a growth mindset in children is one of the most valuable gifts a parent can provide. It's a mindset that empowers them to embrace challenges, learn from failures, and persist in the face of adversity. These traits not only prepare them for financial and entrepreneurial success but also equip them to navigate all aspects of life with confidence and optimism.

The next chapter will explore **the importance of mentorship and networking**, showing how building connections and seeking guidance can open doors to new opportunities and accelerate growth.

Chapter 11:

The Power of Mentorship and Networking

Building Lifelines and Bridges for Your Children's Success

As a father, one of the most rewarding lessons I've taught my kids is this: success isn't achieved alone. Behind every milestone in life, there's usually a mentor guiding the way or a network creating opportunities. I didn't always know this myself—it's one of those things you learn the hard way. But once I understood it, I made it a priority to ensure my children could benefit from mentorship and the value of building genuine connections early on.

Let's talk about how I've approached this as a dad—and how you can too.

What Does a Mentor Mean to a Child?

Think about someone who has helped you navigate life—a teacher, a boss, or even a friend who had wisdom you didn't. That's what a mentor can be for your kids: someone who helps them see possibilities they might not discover on their own.

For my daughter, her passion for art was always there, but it wasn't until I introduced her to a graphic designer friend of mine that she started seeing how her hobby could become a career. That friend didn't just teach her Photoshop tricks; he shared stories about his own journey, the struggles, and the triumphs. Suddenly, she wasn't just doodling; she was designing.

Finding Mentors for Your Kids

Finding the right mentor starts with knowing what excites your child. My son, for example, went through a phase where he was obsessed with mechanics. Every time we passed a garage, he'd point at the cars like they were treasure chests waiting to be unlocked. So, I called up an old buddy who ran an auto shop and asked if my boy could hang around the shop for a few weekends. The experience was transformative. He learned not only how engines work but also the importance of precision and patience.

Here's what worked for me:

1. **Start With Your Network:** Ask yourself, "Who do I know that could inspire or guide my child?" It could be a colleague, a neighbor, or even someone you've met at community events.

2. **Encourage Kids to Seek Guidance Themselves:** As they grow, help them learn to approach mentors independently. Teach them how to introduce themselves, express their interests, and ask thoughtful questions. It's a skill that will serve them well in life.

3. **Look in the Right Places:** If your network doesn't have the right fit, look outside—clubs, organizations, and even social media groups can be great resources for finding mentors.

The Father's Role as the First Mentor

Let's not forget: as fathers, we are often our kids' first and most lasting mentors. They're watching us closely, learning from our habits, our struggles, and how we handle challenges. It's a big responsibility, but it's also a privilege.

For me, this realization hit when I caught my son copying how I managed my budget one day. I'd always thought those late-night spreadsheet sessions went unnoticed, but apparently, he'd been paying attention. That moment reminded me how important it is to model the behavior you want them to adopt.

Sometimes, mentorship is as simple as sharing your stories. I've made it a habit to tell my kids about the mistakes I've made—whether it's about overspending or missing opportunities because I didn't know the right people. It's not about dwelling on the past; it's about showing them how to avoid those same pitfalls.

Networking: A Skill They'll Thank You For
Here's the thing about networking: it's not just about knowing people; it's about building meaningful relationships. This is a lesson I've emphasized with my kids because, in today's world, your network can open doors that no amount of effort can unlock alone.

When my daughter joined a robotics club, I encouraged her to not just focus on the projects but to talk to her teammates and their parents. She hesitated at first—she's shy—but over time, she learned how to share her ideas and listen to others. Those connections eventually led to her joining a summer tech camp, which she absolutely loved.

Here's how I approach teaching networking to my kids:

- **Practice Makes Perfect:** We role-play scenarios where they introduce themselves, talk about their interests, and ask questions.

- **Lead by Example:** I bring them along to social events sometimes so they can see how I interact with people.

- **Create Opportunities:** Whether it's through school activities or community programs, I try to expose them to environments where they can meet others with similar interests.

Why Generosity Matters in Networking

One lesson I always emphasize is that networking isn't just about taking—it's about giving, too. Whether it's helping a friend with a school project or volunteering their time, I encourage my kids to contribute to their relationships.

For instance, when my son started selling homemade bracelets, he also offered to teach his classmates how to make them. That little act of sharing built connections and goodwill, which eventually turned into referrals and more sales. It's a small example, but it shows how giving back strengthens relationships.

Overcoming Challenges in Mentorship and Networking

I won't lie—this isn't always an easy process. Sometimes mentors don't pan out, or networking efforts don't yield immediate results. When that happens, I remind my kids that building relationships takes time and persistence.

One time, my daughter reached out to a local artist for advice, but they were too busy to help. She was disappointed, but I explained that rejection is part of life and encouraged her to keep trying. A few weeks later, she connected with another artist who not only gave her tips but also invited her to a community art exhibit.

Planting Seeds for a Lifetime

Mentorship and networking are like planting seeds—they may not bear fruit immediately, but when nurtured, they grow into something amazing. As fathers, we have the power to guide our children toward these opportunities, teaching them the value of relationships and the wisdom of learning from others.

Remember, the goal isn't just to help them succeed; it's to show them that they don't have to navigate life's challenges alone. With the right mentors and a strong network, they'll have a safety net of support and a wealth of knowledge to draw from as they chase their dreams.

Next, we'll explore **navigating the digital age**, where I'll share how I've helped my kids use technology wisely—balancing its potential with its pitfalls. Stay tuned.

Chapter 12:
Navigating the Digital Age

Guiding Kids to Use Technology Wisely

As a father, watching my kids grow up in a world dominated by screens has been both fascinating and challenging. I didn't have smartphones or the internet when I was their age. Back then, entertainment meant playing outside, reading books, or tinkering with something until it broke—and then figuring out how to fix it. But for my children, technology is their playground, classroom, and sometimes their social circle.

The digital age offers incredible opportunities for learning, growth, and connection, but it also comes with risks and pitfalls. My role as a father isn't just to shield them from the dangers but to equip them with the tools to navigate this digital world responsibly and effectively. Let me walk you through what I've learned about raising kids in this tech-driven era.

Balancing Screen Time and Real Life

Let's face it: the battle over screen time can feel endless. Whether it's gaming, social media, or YouTube, there's always something pulling their attention away from the real world. I used to think the solution was to restrict it altogether, but I quickly realized that's not realistic—or effective.

Instead, I've adopted the philosophy of balance. In our house, screen time is earned. Chores, homework, or time spent outdoors must come first. It's not a punishment; it's about teaching priorities.

One of my proudest moments was when my son chose to spend a Saturday building a model car with me instead of playing his favorite video game. I didn't make him do it—he realized on his own that some offline experiences can be just as fulfilling.

Turning Technology into a Tool for Growth

Technology isn't the enemy; it's a tool. The key is teaching kids how to use it wisely. For instance, when my daughter expressed an interest in photography, I encouraged her to take an online course. It wasn't just about learning a skill—it was about showing her how the internet can be more than entertainment; it can be a resource for growth.

Here are some ways I've turned technology into a positive influence:

1. **Educational Apps and Platforms:** From math games to coding tutorials, there are countless tools out there that make learning fun.

2. **Family Tech Projects:** One weekend, we built a simple website together. It was a great way to bond while teaching them a valuable skill.

3. **Encouraging Creativity:** I've introduced my kids to tools like Canva for design and GarageBand for music production. They've had a blast creating their own projects.

Teaching Online Safety and Digital Responsibility

One of the hardest but most crucial lessons to teach kids is that the digital world isn't always a safe place. As a father, it's my job to ensure they understand the risks without scaring them into avoiding technology altogether.

We've had honest conversations about online predators, scams, and the permanence of what they post online. I've taught them the basics, like not sharing personal information and being cautious about clicking on unknown links.

But beyond safety, I've also emphasized digital responsibility. For example, I once caught my son making a mean comment on a classmate's social media post. Instead of just punishing him, we talked about empathy and the impact of our words—even online. It was a humbling moment for him, and I'm proud to say he's become much more thoughtful since then.

The Pitfalls of Social Media
Social media is a double-edged sword. On one hand, it allows kids to connect with their peers and express

themselves. On the other, it can lead to comparison, insecurity, and even addiction.

I've taken a proactive approach by being involved in my kids' online lives. I know which platforms they use, and we have open conversations about what they see and experience there. For instance, when my daughter felt upset about not getting enough likes on a post, we talked about the value of real-world validation versus virtual approval.

One rule I've set is that screens must be off during family meals and before bedtime. It's a simple way to ensure technology doesn't take over their lives—or mine.

Encouraging a Healthy Relationship with Technology

The goal isn't to eliminate tech from their lives but to help them build a healthy relationship with it. That means teaching them to use it intentionally rather than mindlessly.

For example, when my son wanted a tablet for his birthday, I didn't just hand it over. We made an agreement: he'd use it to learn a new skill—like coding or video editing—at least once a week. To my surprise, he not only kept his promise but also started teaching his younger sister what he'd learned.

Modeling Good Tech Habits

As much as I want my kids to use technology responsibly, I know they're watching how I use it too. If I'm constantly glued to my phone, how can I expect them to be any different?

So, I've made a conscious effort to set an example. When we're spending time together, I put my devices away. I also involve them in my own tech projects, like organizing family photos or exploring new apps for budgeting and planning.

Preparing Them for a Digital Future

The digital age isn't going anywhere, and as a father, I see it as my duty to prepare my kids to thrive in it. By teaching them to balance screen time, use technology as a tool for growth, and navigate the online world responsibly, I'm not just helping them succeed today—I'm equipping them with skills they'll need for the rest of their lives.

Next up, we'll explore **financial independence in adulthood**—how to guide your kids as they transition from financial dependence to standing on their own two feet. Let's dive into one of the most rewarding chapters of parenthood.

Chapter 13:
Guiding Financial Independence in Adulthood

Helping Kids Transition to Financial Autonomy

As a father, there's a unique mix of pride and trepidation that comes when your child begins taking their first steps toward financial independence. It's a monumental shift—from being the one who provides and decides to stepping back and watching them navigate the r own money matters. The journey is both rewarding and challenging, but it's a critical step in preparing them for adulthood.

In this chapter, we'll delve into the lessons, tools, and strategies I've used to help my children transition from being financially dependent to managing their own lives responsibly.

Starting the Conversation Early

The transition to financial independence doesn't begin when your child gets their first job or moves out. It starts much earlier, with conversations about what independence truly means.

I've always emphasized to my kids that financial independence isn't just about earning money—it's about managing it wisely. When my eldest started college, I sat him down for a heart-to-heart. We talked about setting financial goals, living within his means, and understanding the difference between necessities and luxuries.

Setting Realistic Expectations

One of the first things I taught my kids was that independence comes with responsibilities. Bills, rent, groceries—these aren't just abstract concepts; they're real obligations.

To make this lesson hit home, I created a mock budget with them. We included expenses like rent, utilities, transportation, and savings. Seeing the numbers laid out was eye-opening for them. My youngest even joked, "No wonder you always said money doesn't grow on trees!"

Earning Their Own Money

Encouraging kids to earn their own money is a pivotal step toward independence. Whether it's a part-time job, freelancing, or starting a small business, earning teaches them the value of hard work and the rewards of effort.

When my daughter wanted to buy a designer handbag, I saw it as a teaching moment. I told her I wouldn't pay for it, but I'd support her if she wanted to earn the money herself. She took on babysitting gigs, saved diligently, and eventually bought the bag. The pride she felt wasn't just in owning it but in knowing she earned it herself.

Teaching About Debt and Credit

Debt is one of the biggest pitfalls for young adults. Credit cards can be both a blessing and a curse, depending on how they're used. I made it a point to teach my kids about credit early on.

We talked about interest rates, minimum payments, and the dangers of carrying a balance. To illustrate the point, I once showed them how a $500 purchase could balloon into $700 if paid off slowly with interest. It was a powerful visual that stuck with them.

When my eldest got his first credit card, we set some ground rules:

1. Only charge what you can pay off in full each month.

2. Use it to build credit, not to fund a lifestyle.

3. Always keep track of your spending.

Creating a Safety Net

Even as they step into independence, I want my kids to know they're not alone. Life throws curveballs, and having a safety net can make all the difference.

I encouraged each of them to build an emergency fund—enough to cover three to six months of living expenses. To get them started, we set up automatic transfers into their savings accounts. Watching their emergency funds grow gave them a sense of security and accomplishment.

Supporting Big Decisions

As young adults, my kids have faced major financial decisions—buying a car, choosing health insurance, even deciding whether to rent or buy their first homes. While I didn't make these decisions for them, I acted as a sounding board.

When my son was considering leasing a car, we sat down and compared the costs of leasing versus buying. I didn't tell him what to do; I simply gave him the tools to weigh his options. In the end, he chose to buy a used car outright—a decision he later thanked me for.

Encouraging a Growth Mindset

Financial independence isn't a destination; it's a journey. There will be mistakes along the way, and that's okay. I've always encouraged my kids to view setbacks as opportunities to learn and grow.

When my daughter accidentally overdrew her account, she was devastated. Instead of scolding her, I helped her analyze what went wrong and how to avoid it in the future. That experience taught her the importance of keeping a close eye on her balance and planning her spending.

Letting Go (But Staying Involved)

One of the hardest parts of this journey is knowing when to step back. As much as I want to protect my kids from every financial misstep, I've learned that some lessons are best learned through experience.

That doesn't mean I've checked out entirely. I stay involved by checking in periodically, offering advice when asked, and celebrating their successes. When my son paid off his student loans years ahead of schedule, I couldn't have been prouder.

Watching Them Thrive

As a father, there's no greater joy than seeing your kids stand on their own two feet—confident, capable, and secure in their abilities. Helping them transition to financial independence has been one of the most rewarding challenges of my life.

It's not just about money; it's about empowering them to face the world with resilience and confidence. And as I watch them take on new challenges, I'm reminded that the lessons we've shared will serve them well, not just financially but in every aspect of their lives.

In the next chapter, we'll explore how to foster a lifelong love of learning and curiosity—essential traits for adapting to an ever-changing world. Let's dive in.

Chapter 14:
Fostering a Lifelong Love for Learning and Adaptability

Preparing Kids for an Ever-Changing World

As a father, one of the most vital lessons I've strived to teach my kids is that learning doesn't stop at school. The world is constantly evolving—technology advances, industries shift, and new challenges emerge. To thrive in this dynamic environment, they must cultivate curiosity and adaptability.

In this chapter, we'll explore the importance of instilling a lifelong love for learning and how it equips children to embrace change, seek opportunities, and navigate uncertainty with confidence.

Why Lifelong Learning Matters

Life rarely goes according to plan. Careers pivot, industries evolve, and the skills that are valuable today might not be as relevant tomorrow. One of my favorite sayings to my kids is, "The moment you stop learning, you stop growing."

When I was younger, I thought success was about mastering one skill and riding it to the finish line. But life quickly taught me that those who adapt are the ones who thrive. That's the mindset I want to pass on to my children—a belief that every experience, every book, every conversation is an opportunity to learn.

Modeling Curiosity as a Parent

Children learn best by example. If they see you exploring new ideas, asking questions, and challenging yourself, they're more likely to adopt the same mindset.

I made it a habit to share my learning journey with my kids. Whether I was reading a new book, taking an online course, or trying to fix something around the house, I involved them. I'd say, "Let's figure this out together," and we'd dive in, sometimes making mistakes but always learning along the way.

One memorable moment was when I tried to repair our broken washing machine. I didn't have a clue where to start, but I pulled up a YouTube tutorial, gathered some tools, and asked my youngest to assist. It took us hours, and we ended up calling a professional—but the excitement of learning and problem-solving together was priceless.

Encouraging Curiosity in Everyday Life
Fostering curiosity doesn't have to involve grand gestures. It's about encouraging children to ask questions and explore the world around them.

When my kids were younger, I'd often ask, "What do you think?" instead of giving them answers outright. Whether it was about why the sky is blue or how money works, I'd challenge them to think critically and find answers. This habit made them inquisitive and confident in seeking knowledge.

Teaching Adaptability Through Change

Life is full of unexpected twists. Teaching kids to embrace change, rather than fear it, is one of the most important gifts we can give them.

When we had to move cities for work, my children were understandably upset. They were leaving behind friends, schools, and familiarity. I sat them down and explained that change, while uncomfortable, often brings growth. Together, we listed the exciting opportunities this new city might offer—new friends, new experiences, new adventures.

Gradually, they began to see the move as less of a loss and more of a chance to grow. That lesson has stayed with them, helping them navigate other changes with resilience.

Practical Ways to Encourage Lifelong Learning

1. **Expose Them to a Variety of Experiences:**
   Take your kids to museums, libraries, and cultural events. Encourage them to try new activities, whether it's coding, painting, or playing a musical

instrument. The more they're exposed to, the more they'll discover their interests and passions.

2. **Introduce Them to Books and Podcasts:**
I've always been a believer in the power of stories to inspire and educate. Whether it's a novel that sparks their imagination or a podcast that explains complex ideas in simple terms, these resources can open up new worlds for them.

3. **Support Online Learning:**
Platforms like Khan Academy, Coursera, and YouTube offer countless opportunities for kids to learn at their own pace. My eldest learned graphic design through online tutorials and turned it into a side hustle—a skill that continues to serve him today.

4. **Celebrate Their Efforts:**
When my kids took on challenges, whether it was building a science project or learning a new sport, I made sure to acknowledge their effort, not just the

result. This focus on the process taught them to value learning over perfection.

The Role of Failure in Learning

It's important to teach kids that failure isn't the opposite of success—it's part of the journey. I've shared my own failures with my kids, from failed business ideas to financial missteps, to show them that mistakes are learning opportunities.

When my daughter didn't make the school soccer team, she was devastated. But instead of letting her wallow, I encouraged her to reflect on what she could improve and to try again. The next year, she made the team, and the experience taught her the value of perseverance and growth.

Creating a Growth-Oriented Environment at Home

Our homes are the first places where lifelong learning and adaptability are nurtured. Here are some ways I've tried to make our home a hub for curiosity and growth:

- **A "Why Not?" Attitude:** If my kids wanted to explore something new, my default response was, "Why not? Let's give it a shot." This encouraged them to take initiative and try without fear of failure.

- **Family Learning Projects:** From gardening to learning a new language together, we made education a shared experience.

- **Open Discussions:** At dinner, we often discussed current events or debated interesting topics. These conversations sparked critical thinking and kept us all engaged in learning.

Preparing for a Lifelong Journey

As I look at my kids today—confident, curious, and eager to learn—I see the fruits of these efforts. They've embraced the idea that education doesn't stop with a diploma. Whether they're picking up a new hobby, diving into a professional course, or simply asking questions about the world, they're continuing the journey of lifelong learning.

And as a father, that's all I could ever hope for. Because no matter where life takes them, I know they'll have the curiosity to explore, the adaptability to thrive, and the resilience to face whatever comes their way.

In the next chapter, we'll reflect on the power of community—how surrounding our children with the right people and networks can amplify everything we've taught them at home. Let's continue this journey together.

Chapter 15:

The Power of Community—Building a Support Network for Your Kids

It Takes a Village to Raise a Financially Literate Child

As much as I've tried to teach my kids about money, entrepreneurship, and life, I've learned that I can't do it all alone. No parent can. One of the most valuable lessons I've discovered is the importance of community. Surrounding our children with the right people and networks amplifies the values and skills we teach at home.

This chapter explores how to leverage the power of community to nurture financially savvy and well-rounded children. From family and friends to mentors and community programs, we'll dive into how to build a support system that helps your child thrive.

Why Community Matters

There's a saying that's stuck with me: *"You are the average of the five people you spend the most time with."*

The same applies to our children. The people they interact with shape their mindsets, aspirations, and habits.

As a father, I've seen firsthand how mentors, peers, and role models can positively influence my kids. When my eldest started showing an interest in technology, I sought out local coding workshops and introduced him to a neighbor who worked as a software engineer. Those connections inspired him in ways I never could have managed alone.

Creating a Network of Mentors and Role Models

One of the greatest gifts you can give your child is access to mentors—people who've walked the path they aspire to and can provide guidance, encouragement, and inspiration.

1. **Finding Mentors:**
   Look within your circle of family, friends, and colleagues for individuals who can share their knowledge. If your child is interested in business, connect them with an entrepreneur in your

community. If they're curious about art, introduce them to a local artist.

2. **Encouraging Conversations:**
When I introduced my kids to potential mentors, I'd encourage them to ask questions. "How did you get started?" "What challenges did you face?" These conversations not only provided insights but also showed my kids that success is a journey, not an overnight achievement.

3. **Modeling Diversity in Role Models:**
It's important for kids to see role models who reflect their own experiences and also expand their horizons. This could mean connecting them with people from different backgrounds, industries, or walks of life.

The Role of Peers in Learning

Just as mentors can guide, peers can inspire. Children often learn best when they're alongside others who share similar goals and challenges.

When my youngest expressed interest in starting a small baking business, I encouraged her to team up with a friend who loved graphic design. Together, they created a brand, learned about pricing, and handled customer feedback. Watching them collaborate was a reminder that peers can bring out the best in each other.

Leveraging Community Programs and Resources

Many communities offer programs designed to teach kids valuable life skills. From financial literacy workshops to entrepreneurial competitions, these resources can be transformative.

1. **Local Libraries and Community Centers:**
   These often host free or low-cost events, from budgeting classes to STEM activities. I once signed my son up for a financial literacy camp, and he came home teaching *me* about compound interest!

2. **School Clubs and Extracurriculars:**
   Encourage your kids to join clubs that align with their interests, whether it's a business club, robotics

team, or debate society. These groups provide opportunities to learn, lead, and collaborate.

3. **Online Communities:**
In today's digital age, learning communities aren't limited by geography. Platforms like Coursera, Reddit, or even niche Facebook groups can connect kids with like-minded peers and experts.

Teaching Kids to Build Their Own Network

While parents can help lay the groundwork, teaching children how to build their own networks is a skill that will serve them throughout their lives.

1. **Encourage Social Skills:**
Teach your kids the value of introducing themselves, asking questions, and showing genuine interest in others. Whether it's a teacher, a coach, or a neighbor, building relationships starts with connection.

2. **Teach Gratitude:**
I always remind my kids to say thank you, whether

it's for advice, a helping hand, or an opportunity. A simple note of appreciation can leave a lasting impression and strengthen relationships.

3. **Foster Curiosity:**
Encourage your children to be curious about the people they meet. Who are they? What do they do? What can be learned from their experiences? Curiosity opens doors to unexpected opportunities.

Family as the First Community

While external networks are crucial, the family remains a child's first and most enduring community. As a father, I've made it a point to cultivate a supportive, team-like atmosphere at home.

1. **Family Financial Meetings:**
Once a month, we'd sit down as a family to discuss budgets, savings goals, and upcoming expenses. This not only taught my kids about money but also made them feel involved and valued.

2. **Celebrating Wins Together:**
   Whether it was my daughter landing her first babysitting gig or my son saving up for a new gadget, we celebrated their achievements as a family. These moments reinforced the idea that we're all in this together.

3. **Learning Through Shared Projects:**
   From planning a family vacation on a budget to starting a small garden, these projects became opportunities to learn teamwork, problem-solving, and responsibility.

Building a Legacy Through Community

As parents, our ultimate goal is to equip our children with the tools to succeed—not just for themselves, but as contributors to the wider community. A financially literate child grows into an adult who can give back, mentor others, and help build a stronger society.

By surrounding our kids with the right people and networks, we're not just preparing them for individual success; we're empowering them to make a difference in the world.

In the next chapter, we'll reflect on the journey so far and explore how to bring all these lessons together, leaving our children with a solid foundation for a life of financial independence, resilience, and purpose.

Chapter 16:
Reflecting on the Journey—Tying It All Together

What We've Built, and Where We Go From Here

Parenting is a marathon, not a sprint. Teaching children about money, responsibility, and life is an ongoing process—one filled with moments of triumph, occasional setbacks, and countless lessons along the way. As I sit here reflecting on the journey, I realize that the most important part of this process isn't about creating perfection in my kids' lives. It's about planting seeds—seeds that will grow into resilience, independence, and confidence.

This chapter is about looking back on the road we've traveled as parents and forward to the legacy we're building. It's about celebrating the small wins, forgiving the missteps, and trusting that the effort we've poured into teaching our kids will pay off in ways we might not immediately see.

Lessons from the Journey

One thing I've learned as a father is that every step matters, even the imperfect ones. I didn't always know what I was doing—I just knew I wanted to give my children better opportunities and tools than I had growing up.

1. **The Power of Consistency:**
   It's not about grand gestures or perfect execution; it's about showing up. Whether it's having regular conversations about money, sitting down for family budgeting meetings, or cheering on their entrepreneurial experiments, consistency creates habits that stick.

2. **Mistakes Are Part of the Process:**
   Both parents and kids will stumble along the way. I've made financial decisions I regret, and I've watched my kids blow their allowance on something they barely used. But those moments were opportunities to teach—not with judgment, but with patience.

3. **The Little Wins Add Up:**
   I remember the first time my daughter saved

enough to buy her own bike or when my son explained compound interest to a friend. These moments might seem small, but they're evidence that the seeds are taking root.

A Foundation for Independence

Ultimately, the goal of all this work is to raise children who can stand on their own two feet. Financial literacy, entrepreneurship, resilience—they're all pieces of a larger puzzle: independence.

1. **Confidence in Decision-Making:**
   When kids understand the value of money and how to manage it, they approach life's decisions with greater confidence. They're less likely to be swayed by peer pressure or get caught in financial traps.

2. **Freedom Through Financial Security:**
   Teaching our kids to budget, save, and invest isn't just about numbers. It's about giving them the freedom to pursue their dreams without being weighed down by unnecessary financial stress.

3. **Empowering Future Generations:**
   The lessons we teach our children don't end with them. They'll pass on these skills to their own children, creating a ripple effect that can transform families and communities.

Bringing the Family Together

As parents, we often focus on the practical lessons—saving, budgeting, investing—but the deeper value lies in the relationships we build through these experiences.

1. **Shared Goals:**
   Whether it's saving for a family vacation or supporting a cause together, these shared financial goals create a sense of unity and purpose.

2. **Open Communication:**
   By involving kids in financial decisions, we build trust and transparency. They learn to value our guidance and feel confident sharing their own thoughts and concerns.

3. **Celebrating Growth:**
   Reflecting on the progress we've made as a family—no matter how big or small—reinforces the bond between parent and child. It reminds us that we're on this journey together.

Looking Ahead

The journey of teaching our kids doesn't end when they move out or start their own careers. The lessons we've instilled will evolve as they face new challenges and milestones.

1. **Continued Guidance:**
   Even as our children grow into adulthood, we remain a resource and a source of encouragement. Whether it's helping them navigate their first job, buy their first home, or start a family of their own, our influence doesn't stop.

2. **Learning from Our Children:**
   One of the most rewarding parts of this journey has been watching my kids take what they've learned

and make it their own. Sometimes, they even teach me something new—a fresh perspective, a clever idea, or a reminder of the value of curiosity.

3. **Leaving a Legacy:**
   The skills, values, and habits we pass on to our kids are part of a legacy that will outlast us. It's not just about raising financially literate children—it's about contributing to a future generation that's empowered, compassionate, and capable.

A Note to Fellow Parents

To every parent reading this, I want you to know: you're doing enough. The fact that you're here, investing time and energy into equipping your kids for life is a testament to your love and dedication.

There will be days when it feels like nothing is sinking in—when your child shrugs off your advice or makes a decision you don't agree with. But don't lose heart. The seeds you're planting take time to grow. Trust the process.

And remember, you're not alone in this. Lean on your community, celebrate the wins, and forgive yourself for the stumbles. This journey isn't about perfection; it's about progress.

As I close this chapter—and this book—I hope you feel inspired, equipped, and empowered to continue this journey with your kids. Together, we're not just teaching financial literacy; we're raising a generation of thoughtful, resilient, and capable individuals who will shape the future.

So, here's to the lessons, the laughter, and the love that make this journey worthwhile. Thank you for joining me, and I wish you and your family every success as you build your own financial legacy.

A Legacy of Empowerment and Opportunity

As I close this book, I find myself reflecting on the incredible journey we've taken together—not just in these chapters, but in the shared mission to prepare our children for the road ahead. Parenting is never an easy task, and when it comes to equipping our kids with life skills like financial literacy and entrepreneurial thinking, the challenges can feel even greater. Yet, it's in these challenges that the greatest rewards lie.

The work we do as parents is about so much more than teaching dollars and cents. It's about showing our children what's possible when they approach life with knowledge, confidence, and resilience. It's about instilling values that will guide them long after they've left our homes and ventured into the world on their own.

A Future of Possibilities

Through this book, we've explored practical strategies, personal stories, and guiding principles for raising financially savvy, entrepreneurial, and independent kids. From the basics of budgeting to the complexities of investing, from learning through mistakes to celebrating victories, we've built a roadmap for nurturing a new generation of empowered individuals.

But the lessons don't stop here. The most important thing we've learned is that growth is a lifelong process—for our children and for us as parents. The seeds we've planted may take time to bloom, but when they do, they'll bear fruit that lasts for generations.

What Success Really Means

Success as a parent isn't measured by the immediate results of our efforts but by the resilience, wisdom, and compassion we see in our children as they navigate their lives. It's in the way they approach challenges with courage, the way they manage their resources with care, and the way they give back to their communities with generosity.

When we equip our children with the tools to thrive, we're not just giving them a good start in life. We're creating a legacy—one that echoes in their choices, their achievements, and the impact they make in the world.

A Final Note to Parents

If there's one message, I hope you'll carry with you, it's this: you are enough. Your dedication, even in the face of imperfections and uncertainties, is what makes all the difference. The simple act of being present, of trying your best, is what your children will remember most.

The journey of parenting doesn't come with a map, but it's filled with opportunities to learn, grow, and connect. Celebrate the small wins, forgive the stumbles, and trust in the values you've worked so hard to instill.

You are not just raising children—you are shaping the future. And the future is brighter because of the work you're doing today.

Moving Forward

As you close this book, I encourage you to take a moment to reflect on your own journey. Think about the lessons you've already shared with your kids, the ones you're excited to teach, and the ones you'll discover together along the way.

Remember, it's never too early or too late to start building the foundation for a financially secure, independent, and fulfilling life. Take each step with intention, knowing that the effort you put in today will create a ripple effect for years to come.

Thank you for allowing me to be part of your journey. Here's to the incredible future you're building for your children—and the legacy you're leaving behind.

www.ingramcontent.com/pod-product-compliance
Lightning Source LLC
Chambersburg PA
CBHW071550220526
45469CB00003B/971